The Shakespeare Collection

ROMEO AND JULIET

RETOLD BY REBECCA LISLE

Illustrated by Lucy Su

OXFORD
UNIVERSITY PRESS

Character list:

THE HOUSE OF CAPULET

Lord Capulet
(Juliet's father)

Juliet

Nurse
(Juliet's friend and adviser)

Tybalt
(Juliet's cousin)

Paris
(a relative of the prince)

THE HOUSE OF MONTAGUE

Romeo

Lord Montague
(Romeo's father)

Benvolio
(Romeo's friend)

Mercutio
(Romeo's friend)

Friar Lawrence
(Romeo's friend and adviser)

The prince

Long ago in Italy, there were often fights between the great families. Defending the family name was very, very important. The prince of Verona wanted to keep his beautiful city peaceful but it wasn't easy when there were these constant battles. So, when he and his courtiers were walking through the market place one day, he was furious to hear loud voices and the clash of swords. He saw stalls overturned, squashed fruit on the floor, dogs barking and people squabbling.

"Who is responsible for this?" he cried, angrily.

"It's those Capulets and Montagues, my lord!" a flower seller told him, as she gathered up her broken roses and lavender.

The prince was furious.

"I will not tolerate this!" he shouted. "If I catch those families fighting one more time, they will pay for it with their lives!"

The Capulets had run away the moment they saw the prince and now the Montagues fled, too, dodging in and out of the narrow streets.

Among them was Benvolio, a gentle boy, who had been trying to stop the brawl.

"We'd better make ourselves scarce," he urged the others.

"That was magnificent!" laughed one of the brawlers, slipping his dagger back into its sheath and splashing his face with water from the nearby fountain. "I *hate* the Capulets!"

"So do I, of course," said Benvolio, "but brawling in the market place is not dignified."

The Capulets and Montagues had been squabbling for years, in fact for so long they had forgotten what had started the quarrel.

"Oh Benvolio, there you are," said Romeo, meeting his friend shortly afterwards. He sighed. "Come and talk to me and help me to stop thinking about Rosaline."

"Oh, you're not still mooning over her, are you?" laughed Benvolio. "You're always in love with someone!"

"But this is different," argued Romeo. "Rosaline is the most beautiful girl in Verona…"

"Don't tell me, don't tell me," begged Benvolio. "Last week it was Helena, the week before it was Elizabeth…"

"Rosaline is my *true* love," Romeo insisted, "but she won't see me."

"Look," said Benvolio, "Lord Capulet's having a party tonight and there'll be lots of other girls there. Why don't we go?"

"What, gatecrash a Capulet party? Are you *mad*?" Romeo cried.

"Why not?" said Benvolio, calmly. "It's fancy dress and we'll wear masks so no one will recognize us."

So that night, dressed in masks and fine velvet suits, Benvolio, Romeo and his best friend, Mercutio, met outside Lord Capulet's house. It was a grand place with high walls, surrounding large lawns and orchards. The house blazed with lights and the windows were all open. It was easy to creep inside and mingle with the guests.

"Where is Rosaline?" Romeo fretted, peering around. "Where can she b—?"

He stopped suddenly. There, on the other side of the crowded room, was the most beautiful girl he had ever seen. All thoughts of Rosaline instantly vanished.

"Oh, she is glorious!" Romeo sighed, gazing longingly at the girl. "I didn't know what beauty meant until tonight."

He forgot where he was and why, and set off immediately to talk to her and find out who she was.

But Tybalt, Lord Capulet's nephew, recognized him when he began to talk. "That's a Montague voice! It's Romeo. How *dare* he come to our house!" Tybalt raged, storming off angrily. "I won't forget this! I'll pay him back for this outrageous insult!"

But Romeo was blind to everything except
the beautiful girl. He squeezed beside her and
whispered secrets in her ear. They laughed
together and Romeo kissed her… He kissed
her once, and twice, and would have kissed
her again, but suddenly—

"Juliet!" snapped a woman, pulling them
apart. "Come, your mother wants you!"

"Oh, nurse!" cried the girl, running off.
"You spoil everything!"

"Who is her mother?" Romeo asked the old woman.

"Why, the lady of the house, of course!" said the nurse.

"What?" Romeo staggered back. "A Capulet! Disaster! I have fallen in love with my enemy!"

The party was almost over, most of the guests had departed, but Romeo crept into the orchard and hid.

I cannot sleep until I've had one more glimpse of Juliet, he thought. Please, Juliet, please show yourself.

Suddenly a balcony window opened and there was the fair Juliet. She, too, had spoken to her nurse and discovered Romeo was a Montague.

"Oh Romeo, Romeo, why do you have to be a Montague?" she cried to the moon. "But what does a name matter? A rose will still smell sweet whatever name you give it. I love you, Romeo."

Romeo was thrilled! He stepped out of the
dark shadows and called to her...

"Oh, I love you too, Juliet. I know we were
meant for each other. If you really love me,
let's not wait, not a single day!" urged Romeo
passionately. "Let us be married immediately!"

"If you really mean it, I'll agree. But if not,
leave me now."

So the young couple made plans to get married the very next day.

But love had made them very forgetful.

Juliet had forgotten about a certain young man called Paris whom her father had, that very day, decided she was going to marry.

𝒩ext morning, Romeo set off for the
monastery on the edge of Verona where Friar
Lawrence, the wise old priest, lived.

I must persuade the friar to marry us, thought
Romeo, for I cannot live without Juliet. I want to
be with her for ever.

The friar teased Romeo for forgetting about
Rosaline, but then seeing that he was serious
he smiled. "Bless you, my son," he said, "I will
marry you this afternoon. I do believe that a
marriage of love between the two families might
end this age-old quarrel. I wish you luck."

Unfortunately for Romeo, one person who did not wish him luck was Tybalt, Juliet's cousin.

He was busy writing Romeo a letter:

Romeo Montague
You are a villain.
You insulted our family
name by coming to
our house. I challenge
you to a duel. A
duel to death.
Tybalt

He left the letter at Romeo's house, but Romeo never got it, for at that moment, he and Juliet were being married by Friar Lawrence. Romeo gazed into Juliet's eyes and kissed his new bride tenderly.

"How I wish we could be together," he sighed.

"It will be hard to keep this secret," said Juliet. "I want you to come home with me. I want everyone to see my handsome, dear husband!"

"I am certain that is not a good idea," said the friar. "The families have quarrelled for so long, it will be a shock. Wait, and tell them gently."

So Juliet and Romeo embraced each other and kissed sadly.

"Goodbye, my dearest," said Juliet.

"Goodbye, my love!" cried Romeo and slowly he set off for home, dreaming about Juliet and how happy they were going to be.

Suddenly, an angry voice broke into Romeo's thoughts, "Hey there! Villain! Romeo Montague!"

Romeo spun round in surprise. It was Tybalt, brandishing his sword.

"You rat! You lowly coward!" shouted Tybalt. "Draw your sword! I will fight you and kill you right now!"

Romeo shook himself from his dreams and blinked at Tybalt in surprise.

"What's the matter? What have I done?" he asked.

Just then, Mercutio and Benvolio arrived. They quickly took up their places beside Romeo and drew their swords.

"Oh, no, no fighting!" pleaded Romeo. "We're fam—" he stopped. He'd almost told them his secret, that he and Tybalt were related now. He couldn't draw his sword against a member of the family.

"What's the matter with you, Romeo?" hissed
Mercutio. "Tybalt is a rude dog! A crazy Capulet!
Fight him!"

"No, I can't! Please, my friends, let's go,"
Romeo urged desperately.

But Mercutio lunged at Tybalt. Romeo dashed
between them, trying to pull them apart.

"Stop! Please stop!"

"Let me at you!" Tybalt cried, trying to stab
Romeo, but missing and piercing Mercutio
instead, who sank to the ground.

"Are you hurt, Mercutio?" cried Benvolio.

Romeo looked on in despair. "I'm sorry, my dear, best friend! *Mercutio?*" he cried.

But Mercutio was dead.

Romeo, eyes blurred with tears, crazed with sadness and anger, shouting and roaring like a lion, dashed at Tybalt and stabbed him straight through the heart.

Romeo stared at the crumpled, bleeding figure of Tybalt lying at his feet. "Oh, what have I done?" he whispered in disbelief.

"Dead," sighed Benvolio, shaking his head. "You reckless fool! This is serious. The penalty for fighting is death! Come!" Quickly he hurried Romeo away, just as the prince and his men appeared.

I dare not go home, thought Romeo as he ran through the streets, the prince's men will find me! Where can I go? Suddenly he pictured the peaceful monastery and the kindly Friar Lawrence: that was where he would go.

The friar was busy mixing up potions and herbal medicines when a dusty and breathless Romeo arrived.

"I've heard your sorry story already," he told him gently, "but the situation is not as bad as it might be. Since the hot-headed Tybalt started the fight, you are not going to die. Instead the prince has banished you. You must leave Verona."

"But what about Juliet?" cried Romeo.
"I cannot be parted from her!"

"Don't worry," said the friar. "Her nurse has
arranged that you will see Juliet tonight, but
secretly. First thing in the morning you must
go to Mantua until the prince learns of your
marriage and, we hope, forgives you."

So that night Romeo and Juliet kissed each
other and held each other all through the night,
exchanging secrets and soft words of love. But
in the morning…

"Don't go, Romeo, please stay!" Juliet clung to him. "It's still night."

"I'm sure it's light," said Romeo, but he didn't want to open his eyes, he only wanted to stay with his love. "Is that a lark I can hear?" he asked.

"No, no," lied Juliet. "It's still night. It's a nightingale."

But the sun streamed in through the window and Juliet couldn't hold Romeo any longer.

"I must go," said Romeo sadly. "I can't risk anyone finding us together, not yet!"

They kissed each other fondly and said goodbye.

Juliet was so miserable without Romeo, she wandered around the house weeping. She refused to dress or comb her hair.

"What is the matter with you?" snapped her father. "You have nothing to be miserable about. I'll have no more of it!"

But Juliet only wept harder.

"Ridiculous!" cried her father when Juliet broke into tears for the hundredth time that day. "She needs to be married, that's what's wrong with her."

"I've made up my mind, you will soon be married to Paris."

Juliet screamed and wept some more but it only made her father angrier.

"Very well, you will marry *next week!*" he roared.

"Oh, no, Father, *no!*"

"How dare you argue! Then you shall be married this week, on Thursday! And if you don't do as I say, you'll no longer be my daughter!"

Juliet ran to her room and locked herself in.

What could she do? Who would help? The only person she could think of was Friar Lawrence...

Juliet wept angrily as she told the friar of her parent's marriage plans for her.

"It would be a sin to marry twice," said the priest, taking her hand. "I know you love Romeo, so I have a proposal: drink this potion the night before you are due to marry. It will put you to sleep and in the morning you will appear to be dead. I will tell Romeo our plan. He will be waiting when you wake and then you can run away to Mantua."

On the day that Juliet was to marry Paris, her nurse woke the household with an awful scream.

"Juliet is dead! Juliet is dead!"

Everyone rushed into Juliet's room and there she lay, her beautiful face as white as chalk, no breath passing her lips, no thudding of her heart.

"It's all my fault!" cried her father, sobbing. "I should not have forced her to marry!"

The entire Capulet family were stricken with sadness and remorse.

As was the custom, they dressed Juliet in her finest clothes and lay her on a stone slab in the family chapel.

The terrible news spread quickly and it soon reached Romeo in Mantua. Unfortunately, Romeo had never received the friar's message.

"Juliet Capulet is dead!"

Romeo heard the awful words. Juliet! *Dead?* He sank to the floor.

"My darling, my dearest!" he cried. "What use is life to me now, without you? It is nothing! *Nothing!* Oh, Juliet, I shall join you. We'll be together in death."

Romeo went straight out to buy himself
a terrible poison, so strong that just one drop
could kill twenty men.

*I*n the dark of night, Romeo crept through
the gardens to the Capulet chapel to find his
dear love. It was very quiet. Inside the chapel,
candles burned, their flickering shadows lighting
up the white lilies that had been placed around
the room.

At the far end, on a big stone slab, lay Juliet.

Romeo walked slowly towards her. "O my love!
My wife! Still so beautiful!"

Feasting his eyes on her for the last time,
Romeo lay down beside her.

"Goodbye, my love." He took the poison and
gave her a final kiss. "So with a kiss I die," he
muttered as the deadly poison coursed through
his body.

Only a few moments later, Juliet woke up.

She shivered to find herself in the cold chapel, then remembered the friar's clever plan. A smile began to form on her lips, but it instantly froze as she saw Romeo.

He was so still. So very still, with deadly poison in his hand.

"Oh! Romeo!" she cried. "True poison this
time! My life is nothing without you! Quickly,
quickly, let me take some, too."

She took the bottle from his hand and tried
to drink from it, but there wasn't a drop.

"Oh, there's no poison left to help me follow
you. But I will join you, Romeo, I will."

But how?

Finding Romeo's dagger, Juliet grabbed it
gratefully and plunged it into her heart.

When the Capulets and Montagues found the two young people dead and learnt from the friar that they were married, they were laid low with grief.

"This is all because of our fighting and quarrelling," wept Lord Capulet.

"We must stop this hatred before any more young lives are wasted," agreed Lord Montague, with a heavy heart.

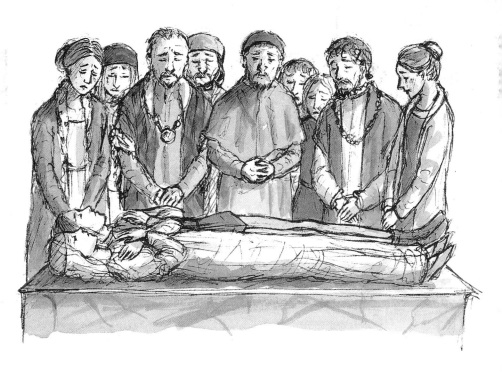

Lord Capulet took his hand in friendship
and they agreed to raise a statue to honour
the love of their children. There was peace
in Verona at last.

Then the prince of Verona stepped forward
and summed up what everyone was thinking,
saying, "there never was a story of more woe
than this of Juliet and her Romeo."